Snowshill Man

Gloucestershire

THE NATIONAL TRUST

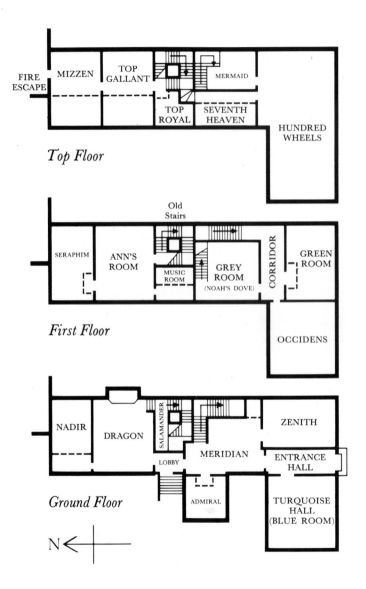

Top Floor

FIRE ESCAPE

MIZZEN

TOP GALLANT

MERMAID

TOP ROYAL

SEVENTH HEAVEN

HUNDRED WHEELS

First Floor

Old Stairs

SERAPHIM

ANN'S ROOM

MUSIC ROOM

GREY ROOM (NOAH'S DOVE)

CORRIDOR

GREEN ROOM

OCCIDENS

Ground Floor

NADIR

DRAGON

SALAMANDER

LOBBY

MERIDIAN

ADMIRAL

ZENITH

ENTRANCE HALL

TURQUOISE HALL (BLUE ROOM)

N

CONTENTS

Snowshill Manor

Snowshill Manor was owned by Winchcombe Abbey from 821 until the dissolution of the monasteries in 1539 when it passed to the Crown. Thereafter it has had many owners and tenants, and had become a semi-derelict farm by 1919 when it was bought and restored by Charles Paget Wade. The visitor to Snowshill Manor can enjoy three distinct features of the property:

The House is a typical traditional Cotswold manor house built of local stone. Although the south front displays classical details of c.1720, the main part of the house is of c.1500, altered and extended c.1600. The west front, towards the garden, with its small mullioned windows clearly indicates the earlier style.

The Contents were collected entirely by Mr Wade from 1900 until 1951 when he gave them with the manor to the National Trust. Charles Wade was an architect, artist and craftsman from Yoxford in Suffolk, who inherited from his father sugar estates in the West Indies. This enabled him to devote his life to amassing his enormous and varied collection of craftsmanship which he acquired mainly from antique shops and dealers. He spent many hours in the manor house arranging and restoring his collection, whilst living in the old cottage in the courtyard.

The Garden with terraces and ponds was laid out by Mr Wade between 1920 and 1923 on the site of the old farmyard and contains various garden ornaments and a profusion of colourful and scented flowers and plants.

I have not bought things because they were rare or valuable, there are many things of every day use in the past, of small value, but of interest as records of various vanished handicrafts. What joy these old things are to live with, each piece made by the hand of a craftsman, each has a feeling and individuality that no machine could ever attain.

A room can be filled with innumerable things and yet have a perfect atmosphere of repose, if they are chosen with thought and care so as to form one harmonious background. The furniture should not stand out as a series of silhouettes, but merge into the background, the highlights being sufficient to show its form.

This collection, not a museum, will be a valuable record in days to come.

C.P.W. 1945

Charles Wade at Snowshill, c.1940

The south front of the house

Charles Wade, 1883-1956

Charles Wade as a young boy

Snowshill Manor, as the visitor sees it today, is the creation of one man, the architect, artist-craftsman, collector and poet Charles Paget Wade.

Wade was a solitary, but happy child. His childhood was a magical time when the textures and colours of everyday objects could be enjoyed with an innocent relish, as he recalled nostalgically in his memoirs, *Days Far Away*: 'Here was a Kingdom beyond the ken of Grown-Ups, all free from that overlooking eye. This happy realm of under the table and round the skirtings. How intimate one was with the legs of furniture, textures and patterns of carpets.' Even the labels of the stock in his toy haberdasher's shop were the stuff of poetry – 'Osnabury', 'Shaloon', 'Kersey', 'Bombazine', 'Wincey', 'Tiffany'.

Cantonese cabinet of c.1720 in Zenith. It belonged to Charles Wade's grandmother and fascinated him as a small boy

At seven life became more spartan, when Wade was sent to live with his grandmother, Katherine Spencer, in Great Yarmouth: 'seldom any laughter, and never any visitors or young folk'. In search of excitement he explored the seashore, watching the roll of incoming waves and the scuttle of crabs. Fortune-tellers, booths selling 'all manner of useless objects, inscribed "A Present from Yarmouth"', Punch and Judy shows, the wrought-iron nails in the tarred wooden pier – all delighted him: 'the days were never too long, winter or summer, indoors or out'.

In his grandmother's austere drawing-room was a Chinese cabinet (now in Zenith), which he found endlessly fascinating. 'Only on Sundays were the doors allowed to be set open and as they opened out came the fragrance of camphor, then the interior of this Enchanted Golden Palace was revealed, a Palace fit for the greatest Mandarin ... There was a little wax angel with golden wings from a Christmas tree when Grannie was a child. Two musical boxes which played airs with notes like ripples and clear cascades of falling waters. A little bone model of a "Spinning Jenny" with two bone ladies,' and much else. The contents of this cabinet inspired Wade to become a collector and to create on a vaster scale his own 'cabinet of curiosities' at Snowshill.

Wade seems to have spent the greater part of his schooldays, in Yarmouth, Eastbourne, and lastly Uppingham, day-dreaming: 'I would be planning out great works for the holidays such as how to build a punt for our pond or a little house on piles over the river; the margins of all my lesson books were filled with sketches of such things.' The only subjects that held his attention were drawing and carpentry. Mr Blogg, the carpenter at St Andrew's School, Eastbourne, encouraged Wade's natural talent for woodworking, and he rapidly acquired the skills he was to put to such good use in restoring Snowshill and the collections with which he filled it.

Wade left school determined to be an architect. He was articled to E.F. Bisshopp in Ipswich, a town which he found shared many of the charms of Great Yarmouth. Bisshopp was not an inspiring mentor (the hardest of 4H pencils was all that he allowed at the drawing-board), but study of the town's ancient timber houses made Wade an expert architectural draughtsman.

Having qualified as an Associate of the Royal Institute of British Architects in 1907, Wade joined the firm of Parker & Unwin, then among the leading exponents of the Arts and Crafts Movement, and the architect of Hampstead Garden Suburb. Raymond Unwin gathered around him a group of outstanding young architects, including M.H. Baillie Scott who was later to help Wade transform the garden at Snowshill. Wade seems to have been employed principally for his skill in producing seductive presentation drawings decorated with borders of silk, ribbon and mother-of-pearl.

The death of Wade's father in 1911 brought him a private income from the family estates in St Kitts in the West Indies, and enabled him to leave Parker & Unwin where he had grown increasingly frustrated at having to provide for clients' needs in his designs. Like Michelangelo, he said, 'No fee, no interference'. In the years leading up to the First World War Wade concentrated

Above:
The drawing-room in the home of Wade's grandmother

THE HARNESS ROOM.

Watercolour of the harness room in the coach house of the Wade family home at Yoxford in Suffolk

on book illustration. For Kate Murray's *The Spirit of the House* he produced precise but delicate line drawings which do much to evoke the atmosphere of the imaginary country house that is the subject of the book. With the same mixture of imagination and craftsmanship Wade also created a model village, complete with station and clockwork train, for Kate Murray's daughter, Elizabeth.

During the First World War Wade served, appropriately, in a workshop company of the Royal Engineers. Even amid the chaos of the Western Front he was able to exercise his talents as carpenter and interior designer: 'I lined the interior [of the Orderly Room] with "sand bag" hessian and made neat shelves and a cupboard for Army papers. I also hung up a few pictures,

made a shelf for my books and even got a pleasing cover for my bunk.' Back numbers of *Country Life* provided a further diversion from the war. While he was leafing through the property pages one day in the field canteen, an advertisement for Snowshill Manor caught his eye. On leaving the army, he found the house still on the market and in 1919 decided to buy it.

The Cotswolds were at the time the natural destination for someone with Wade's interest in traditional English craftsmanship. In 1902 C.R. Ashbee had moved his short-lived Guild of Handicraft to nearby Chipping Campden, and the following year the furniture-makers Ernest Gimson and Sidney and Ernest Barnsley had set up their workshops in Sapperton. Wade found Snowshill in a ruinous state

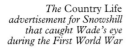

The Country Life *advertisement for Snowshill that caught Wade's eye during the First World War*

Wade's delightful watercolour of a child's Christmas presents under the tree

8

*Charles Wade in Cromwellian armour
on the steps of Snowshill*

amid a jungle of rampant nettles, but had the imagination to see what it might become. With a gang of 28 workmen he embarked on a complete restoration of the house, taking great care to preserve as much of the old panelling and stonework as he could. He then set about filling it with his extraordinary collection.

Inspired by his grandmother's 'wonderful cabinet', Wade, at the age of seven, had begun buying small curios out of his pocket money, and the collecting fever never left him. In an age before the antique shop had been invented, Wade's 'hunting trips' with his great friend Commander Fred Hart took him to many out of-the-way places. From dusty attics and narrow back alleys he rescued the forgotten mementoes of another age: 'over all a certain sadness lies, for all have seen fairer days. Time when each piece was brought home with pride, cared for, treasured and loved. Now all sadly neglected lies, forlorn and covered in dust.' Wade carried off his new discoveries to the workshop where they were carefully restored and then found an appropriate setting at Snowshill. At first he collected simple, mainly English, household objects, but he became increasingly adventurous, pursuing painted European furniture and Far Eastern craftsmanship to create ever more dramatic and colourful tableaux. The dazzling collection of Japanese armour, which now dominates the Green Room, came from all over England. Some of the suits were found in a plumber's shop in Cheltenham, some in Cheshire, while others were unearthed from a dusty heap in a cellar off Charing Cross Road.

The atmosphere of Wade's cottage at Snowshill in the 1930s is perfectly summed up by his friend, Richard Kayll: 'The house was dark and scented. The pungent smell of wood smoke and sharp tang of turpentine and oil lamps impinged on the nose. Here were no carpets or carpet beaters, no photographs or pictures, no fountain pens or blotters, no coal so no scuttle, in fact none of the paraphernalia I was used to. A painted wooden cat, a leather porter's chair, a trundle chair on wheels like a trolley with drawer beneath, spits, bundles of old umbrellas racked overhead, glass apothecaries' jars reflecting sharp points of light from polished steel and brass in this room of Rembrandt half tone and shadow differed from anything I had experienced.'

To this unique atmosphere Wade himself added a touch of drama, often startling his guests by materialising noiselessly from a dark corner. He adored dressing up from among his vast collection of old costumes, and striking suitably Irvingesque poses. Visitors to Snowshill, who included John Betjeman, Virginia Woolf, Clough Williams-Ellis, Graham Greene and J.B. Priestley, were often roped into amateur theatricals, both in the garden and the house. Wade's friend, the Edwardian architect Sir Albert Richardson, was a particularly enthusiastic participant, as his grandson, Simon Houfe, recalls: 'Among the favourite sketches were "The Last Night in the Condemned Hold" with horrifying groans and oaths and the dragging of chains across the floor and "The Wives of Wapping Welcoming Home Nelson's Sailors" for which my grandfather turned

A corner of Snowshill, as drawn by Wade

female impersonator in falsetto cockney. Probably the most spine-tingling of these masques was the one about the "Plague Year". For this the house was completely darkened and nothing could be heard but the distant footfall of my grandfather as he paced the extremities of the house with swinging lantern, knocking on doors, opening them on creaky hinges and intoning menacingly "Bring out your dead! Bring out your dead!"

In 1946 Wade married and he spent many of his remaining years in the West Indies. He retained a lively interest in Snowshill, continuing to add to his collection. In 1951 he presented the house and its contents to the National Trust, having completed negotiations in 1938. At the hand-over ceremony in 1952 Wade was the same unmistakable figure, 'still mischievous, waxy complexioned, a medieval face seen through the wood smoke'.

Wade died in July 1956 and is buried with his mother and sisters in Snowshill churchyard.

The living-room of the Priest's House where Wade would sit listening to Much Binding in the Marsh *on his battery-driven wireless*

The History of Snowshill

From 821 until the dissolution of the monasteries in 1539 Snowshill Manor belonged to the Abbey of St Mary at Winchcombe. During the latter sixteenth century the manor passed through many hands, belonging briefly to the Crown and members of the nobility, but it is doubtful whether any of those owners actually visited the manor. Indeed for much of its subsequent history Snowshill was owned by absentee landlords.

The northern end of the manor house is the oldest part of Snowshill, having been built around 1500 as a traditional medieval house with a great hall. The only external sign to survive is the large chimneybreast on the east front, which serves the great fireplace in Dragon. The ceilings of Ann's Room and Seraphim also date from this period.

About 1600 the great hall seems to have been divided horizontally and vertically to provide more conveniently sized rooms, and the house extended southwards. The result was a long building of two storeys with large attics above and stone gables at each end; that at the north still survives. The main front faced west across the valley with a doorway at its centre, reached by a flight of stairs. Both still remain beside the small room added later. The traditional Cotswold stone mullioned windows date from this alteration, as does the steeply pitched stone-tiled roof.

The internal partition walls are all of timber studding which makes dating the history of alterations difficult. The present form of most of the rooms, windows and fireplaces dates from around 1600 and many of the old doors and frames can be seen incorporated in Mr Wade's restorations.

The Old Stairway, built within the hall when it was subdivided, is worthy of inspection, as it is of a simple construction of naturally crooked timbers resting one on another round a square well.

On St Valentine's Eve, 1604, the secret marriage of Ann Parsons to Anthony Palmer took place in one of the rooms carved out of the old great hall, now known as Ann's Room. Ann Parsons, related by marriage to John Warren, at that time the owner of Snowshill, was taken from the home of her guardian by Palmer and his friends and brought to Snowshill Manor where she was married at midnight by the vicar of nearby Broadway. The marriage was subsequently declared invalid. There is no reason to doubt the facts, but the story has over the years acquired the patina of legend and must have appealed to Charles Wade's sense of the dramatic.

Left: *Watercolour by Wade of the west front of the house*

Far left: *Ann's Room, the setting for the midnight marriage of Ann Parsons and Anthony Palmer on St Valentine's Eve, 1604*

In the early part of the eighteenth century, William Sambach and his son, also named William, owned and lived at Snowshill as true Lords of the Manor, making an impression on both the house and the village. They were buried in the church and a tablet to the son states that 'he was a zealous friend of the church with a true interest in this country [county]'.

In about 1720 the Sambachs seem to have decided to change the orientation of the house by adding one room at each level to the south-west corner and a new main door with the Sambach arms in the pediment above, to give the impression of a small Georgian house facing south.

The small 'gazing room' (Admiral) was also added to the west side. These additions contrast with the earlier work on the outside by being built of yellow-coloured stone and having sash windows. The prominent hipped stone-tiled roof across the new south front replaced the gable that would have terminated the earlier building. The mullioned and transomed windows of this were, however, retained, and the purlins that were cut back to form this roof can still be seen in Hundred Wheels.

The new rooms were fitted with painted softwood panelling and small iron fire grates. These features were also fitted to the Green Room and the Grey Room in the earlier structure where they still survive. The front stairs were also formed to give more convenient access to the new rooms of the south front. At some later time several windows on the east side were blocked up, probably due to the window tax. Mr Wade did not re-open them as he favoured sub-dued lighting and especially disliked a room that had windows on more than one side.

The manor was bought by Samuel Blackwell in 1759 at a local auction, but he did not live there long. From 1779, when the Manor was sold to John Small of Clapham, the first of a series of absentee landlords, the house was occupied by tenant farmers until 1919, when it was purchased by Charles Wade. During this period there were no further alterations made to the house, except for the addition of a stable to the north end in 1889, which has been converted into the administrator's cottage. At the same time, the estate was divided into several farms that were successively sold off, so that the house came to Mr Wade with only 14 acres and the option on the home farm, which he did not take up.

The manor house had deteriorated to the condition of a semi-derelict farmhouse, suffering from damp and serious structural decay when Mr Wade bought it. He then began a large-scale restoration in the spirit of William Morris at Kelmscott and the Barnsleys at nearby Sapperton. He removed the plaster ceilings from most of the rooms, moved partitions back to their original places, unblocked fireplaces and fitted contemporary oak panelling to many of the rooms, to recapture the Tudor atmosphere in the early part of the house. Charles Wade scorned the use of electricity and modern conveniences, and, although not living in the manor, he did entertain in Dragon, where theatricals were performed from the gallery to audiences before the great log fire.

Charles Wade in 1909, wearing one of the costumes with which he was to entertain visitors to Snowshill

View from the garden towards Snowshill church, in which William Sambach and his son lie buried. The Sambachs lived at Snowshill in the early eighteenth century

TOUR OF THE HOUSE

Above: *Watercolour of the market in Great Yarmouth remembered by Wade from his happy childhood*

Left: *Seraphim*

Tour of the House

The Exterior

The south front is approached by way of the small lodges, formerly used as stables, and through two forecourts, separated by a fine pair of gate piers of *c*.1720. These piers, together with iron railings which have disappeared, represent the original road boundary of the property. From here the front has a handsome but irregular appearance: to the right mullioned and transomed windows of *c*.1600, and to the left sash windows of *c*.1720, the last major building period. In the centre is a pedimented doorway with the arms of William Sambach who formed the south front in the early eighteenth-century.

The south front of the house, showing the fine early eighteenth-century gate piers

The Interior

The names of the rooms, chosen by Mr Wade, usually bear some relation to their contents, their decoration or their position in the house. In this short guidebook it is only possible to refer to some of the principal objects of this varied and extensive collection. These are listed in each room in a sequence from the left of the door, but are liable to minor alterations.

Entrance Hall

The Entrance Hall dates from the remodelling of the south front in *c*.1720 and has been the main entrance since then.

CONTENTS

An iron strong box, commonly known as an Armada Chest, which has a complicated locking mechanism operated by one key in the centre of the lid. It has a dummy keyhole in the front of the box and two hasps for padlocks. Seventeenth-century German.

A large oak hanging cupboard.

A hall porter's chair with hood, eighteenth-century.

Portrait of Charles Wade at the age of sixty-eight in 1951 by his friend Mrs K. Browning, wife of the vicar of St Kitts.

Coats of arms including members of the Wade family in the sixteenth and seventeenth centuries and of Henry VIII, former owner of the manor.

Delft tiles depicting biblical subjects.

Turquoise Hall (Blue Room)

This room is also of about 1720 and has the original fireplace and softwood panelling, repainted by Mr Wade.

CONTENTS

In the centre of the room is a very finely made Japanese painted wood figure of a carver of masks, signed 'Hananuma', made for European tourists in the late nineteenth century. A similar figure, the basket seller, can be seen next to the door.

In the large glass case is a ship model of the frigate HMS *Romulus*, a fifth-rate ship of the line with 44 guns. Built by Adams at Buckler's Hard in Hampshire, it was launched on 17 December 1777. *Romulus* was captured off Chesapeake Bay by the French ship *Eville* on 19 February 1781.

On the window sill are two Chinese musical instruments, a dulcimer (Yang-Qin) and a mouth organ (Sheng).

A bone model of a Canton flower boat.

Five Japanese clocks, two pillar clocks with the time shown by a pointer on a vertical scale, a lantern clock, a pillar clock with a sliding scale, and, in the bureau, a bracket clock with date chapters. Before 1873 Japanese time was divided into six periods of daylight and six of darkness, which varied with the seasons.

A Chinese lacquered bureau made for export to Europe *c*.1720 with three large shaped drawers below and the upper cabinet surmounted by a broken shaped pediment.

A large cabinet which has a tortoiseshell front, with brass inlay and semi-precious stones, *c*.1850. A type of architectural furniture much favoured in Italy in the sixteenth century.

A Chinese cabinet of black and gold lacquer in the form of a Buddhist shrine. This type of cabinet was made in Canton for export to Europe in the eighteenth century. They were often packed with tea, porcelain or silks, as transport from China was then very expensive.

A figure of a Japanese wind spirit, mounted on the original softwood panelling in the aptly named Turquoise Hall

A Japanese wood figure of a carver of masks, signed 'Hananuma' (Turquoise Hall)

Meridian

Meridian derives its name from its central position in the house. In this and other rooms the oak panelling is mostly Tudor. Mr Wade bought a quantity of this and had more made and fitted to match. He also removed the plastered ceiling to expose the oak beams and floor joists.

CONTENTS

On the window sill is an early seventeenth-century Spanish cabinet known as a Papileira, on which stands a model of a cutter *c.*1900, and at the sides two Burmese red lacquer temple rice jars.

A highly decorated walnut cabinet, Italian, *c.*1660.

A model of a Dutch yacht with leeboards, *c.*1800.

Two seventeenth-century Flemish tapestries.

An English seventeenth-century oak bread cupboard, on which stands a sixteenth-century Spanish reliquary in the form of a bust of St Ignatius of Loyola (1491–1566), founder of the Jesuit movement.

Over the door to the stairs are a blunderbuss by W. Henshaw, Strand, London, *c.*1740, and three court or small swords with fine cut steel hilts, English eighteenth-century.

A Belgian gilt processional reliquary.

Two drums of about 1800, the smaller said to have been used at the Battle of Waterloo.

Two Venetian gilt lanterns and a church tabernacle.

An Italian cabinet of red tortoiseshell, *c.*1700.

A sedan chair with the French royal emblems *c.*1760 from the Château de Marly.

A red lacquer longcase clock by Stephen Rimbault, London, *c.*1770.

A series of heraldic banners including those of the Duke of Cambridge and the Duke of Kent from St George's Chapel, Windsor.

Zenith
This room is of about 1600 and with its original fireplace was incorporated into the new south front of 1720. The panelling is similar to that in Meridian.

CONTENTS
High in the wall is a blocked window converted by Mr Wade into a niche with doors on which are painted a hymn to the Virgin Mary.

Still-life with a basket of fruit, painting by Jacques Linard (*c.*1600–45), one of the first French artists to adopt the Netherlandish speciality of still-lifes.

Daghestan rug and Salor Turkoman and Yomud tent bags.

On the left when entering is the cabinet which belonged to Charles Wade's grandmother, and was the start of his fascination with objects of craftsmanship.

Flemish bracket clock with paper dial, *c.*1700.

A Chinese shrine cabinet similar to those in the Turquoise Hall.

High in the east wall of Zenith, Wade converted a blocked window into this niche, on whose doors are painted a hymn to the Virgin Mary and the Wade family coat of arms

Left: *Meridian is at the centre of the house. Shown here are an Italian cabinet of red tortoiseshell, a sedan chair and a Belgian reliquary*

Over the fireplace is a portrait of a man, Dutch, seventeenth-century.

Friesland bracket clock with a single weight working the movement and the strike, *c.*1700.

A leather-covered travelling box, English seventeenth-century.

A clavichord, nineteenth-century copy of an original dated 1533.

An iron chest similar to the one in the Entrance Hall. The decorative metal strips would prevent the contents of the box becoming entangled with the mechanism when the key was turned. Seventeenth-century.

Tavern clock *c.*1785 from Braintree, Essex, of the type used in coaching inns, market halls and public places. Also known as 'Act of Parliament' clocks, because of a tax introduced in 1797 to raise revenue for the Napoleonic Wars. Many people relied on them at a time when clocks were being concealed to avoid payment of the tax. The effect of the Act on the horological business was so disastrous it was repealed after nine months.

The Holy Family, copy of a painting by Andrea del Sarto.

Zenith dates from c.1600. Here are shown Chinese shrine cabinets, a tavern clock of c.1785 and a Daghestan rug

Admiral

A small room of *c.*1720, with fitted cupboards and a corner fireplace, it contains a large collection of objects, mainly of nautical interest.

CONTENTS

A brass 5½ inch-calibre landservice mortar dated 1794. This type, known as the Royal Mortar, was in continuous use from 1750 to 1850.

A collection of decorative smoking pipes and tobacco boxes.

A collection of pocket globes in cases, early nineteenth-century.

Customs officers' slide-rules, late eighteenth-century.

A model of an armed ketch of about 1700.

Two brass tiller yokes in the shape of dolphins from the rudders of ships' boats.

A narwhal tusk and two walking sticks of the same material.

Several other walking sticks including one containing a telescope.

A collection of eighteenth- and nineteenth-century naval swords, including that of Mr Wade's great friend, Commander Hart, 1908.

Orreries and planetaria showing the position of the planets in relation to the sun, early nineteenth-century.

Eighteenth- and nineteenth-century telescopes.

Eighteenth-century sand glasses, ¼, ½ and 1 hour.

A model of a Cornish lug-rigged fishing boat by Mr Wade.

A back-staff 1746, four octants *c.*1800 and a sextant *c.*1850.

A Culpeper-type microscope in original box, *c.*1750.

Various compasses and other navigational and surveying instruments.

Three miniature ship models of wood made by French prisoners-of-war, *c.*1810.

English and Chinese porcelain.

A corner of Admiral

Admiral houses Wade's extensive collection of nautical and scientific objects

Front Staircase (Ascendens)

The stairs were built in *c*.1720 to give access to the new rooms formed at that time.

CONTENTS

Portrait of Mr Wade aged twenty-seven by Thomas Roberts, 1910.

Portrait of George Digby, 2nd Earl of Bristol (1612–76/7)?, copy of a painting by van Dyck. Digby was an adviser of Charles I and II, and renowned for his good looks.

Equestrian portrait of William III.

Portrait of Sir Thomas Aston (1550–1613), dated 1603. Charles Wade may have bought the painting when Aston Hall was demolished in 1938.

A dockyard model of a forty-gun frigate *c*.1800, repaired by Mr Wade.

A weather prognosticator 1831 and a perpetual almanac 1801.

The inscription at the top of the stairs means:

> *For me today*
> *For him tomorrow*
> *After that, who knows?*

Corridor

CONTENTS

English and Continental lace bobbins.

Samples of lace, mainly Bedfordshire-Maltese, mostly late nineteenth-century to earlier patterns. The lower framed collection of lace is much earlier and finer.

The side of a coach with the arms of the Countess Cowper.

A leather-covered travelling box shaped to fit on a coach roof.

Watercolour of a Chinese nobleman.

A barrel organ by Gerok, *c*.1810, which belonged to Charles Wade's great-great-grandmother, Bridget Lloyd.

Green Room

The Green Room contains a very remarkable collection of twenty-six suits of Japanese Samurai armour of the seventeenth to nineteenth centuries, gathered from various parts of England between the years 1940–45. Mr Wade arranged the room to give the impression of a company of warriors meeting in the gloom with their weapons, banners and an assortment of sacred and domestic objects around them.

On the left is a very fine Japanese Buddhist shrine or Butsudan with folding doors and screens, containing various bronze and lacquer objects.

On the right is another smaller Butsudan, on which stands an Egyptian aragonite alabaster unguent pot. Protodynastic, 4000–3500 BC.

Left and right:
Details of three of the Japanese Samurai warriors in the Green Room. There are 26 suits of armour in all, dating from the seventeenth to nineteenth centuries

Occidens

This room dates from the additions in *c*.1720, and contained, until 1982, over two thousand items of costume collected by Charles Wade. These have been removed to environmentally controlled storage and are currently not available for study.

Some cabinets now contain many of Mr Wade's own drawings and paintings, together with houses and the harbour from the model village once in the garden. Others have changing displays from the reserve collections and it is hoped that a few items of costume may be on show in the future.

The cabinets are illuminated with fibre optic lighting units and are at the optimum levels to preserve the many kinds of object on show.

Objects on display in Occidens

Grey Room (Noah's Dove)

This room has painted panelling of *c*.1720 similar to the Turquoise Hall, although the window is earlier.

CONTENTS

On the window sill are models of an Indian oxcart, a brightly painted Sicilian carreto and a Naples wine cart, and also two English pharmaceutical machines for rolling out pills by hand.

A red lacquer clock by Philip Barnard, London *c*.1760.

A Flemish oak canopied bed *c*.1700 but with additions dated 1825. This bed, like the one in Ann's Room, is actually six feet long although it looks shorter.

On the bed is an English cottage patchwork quilt of *c*.1850.

A harp by Delveau, early nineteenth-century.

A Chinese export sewing box, late nineteenth-century, complete with ivory needlecases, bobbins etc.

A collection of eighteenth- and nineteenth-century drinking and other glasses including a fine set of six Jacobite wine glasses *c*.1750 inherited by Mr Wade from his family, in a red lacquer cabinet.

Ascend the staircase to

Mermaid

This room and Seventh Heaven adjoining would originally have been one, part of the attic storey formed in the alterations to the hall house *c*.1600.

A section of the large doll's house in Mermaid, which contains various eighteenth- to nineteenth-century dolls and toy soldiers, as well as a complete model shop with its proprietor 'Robert', one of Wade's favourite childhood toys

CONTENTS

A framed print of a First Class, First Rate Line of battle Ship of 131 guns, with a screw propeller and auxiliary steam power, designed by Charles Lewis Pickering *c*.1852.

A doll's house made by Wade and fully furnished with nineteenth-century furniture, inhabited by Lord Mex and his family.

A large doll's house containing various eighteenth- to nineteenth-century dolls, soft toys, model soldiers and a complete model shop, with its proprietor, 'Robert'.

A model of a patent churn, by J. Thorian, 1844.

A collection of wax and plaster dolls in a glass case.

A framed collection of late eighteenth-century watch cocks.

A sack barrow from a windmill.

Hundred Wheels

This is the attic of the new south front of *c*.1720, but contains many earlier beams re-used. It had been used as a granary, and now contains objects mainly connected with transport.

CONTENTS

A model of a windmill fitted as a very elaborate wind toy with soldiers performing various movements when the sails turn.

A sedan chair, which may be converted to a brouette with the use of the wheels and shafts seen above it.

Two coach builder's sample models, a barouche painted yellow and a Blessington coach, painted blue.

A Bath chair.

Three- and four-wheeled pedal-operated vehicles of a kind made experimentally and unsuccessfully between 1825 and 1865.

A collection of twelve 'boneshaker' bicycles of 1870–85, including one made of iron by the Chipping Campden blacksmith, others

A model windmill based on the type common c.1600. When the sails turn, the soldiers perform elaborate manoeuvres

with wooden wheels and one with a wooden frame.

A hobby-horse c.1820, the earliest form of bicycle without pedals, but with an elbow rest and footrests for free-wheeling downhill.

A fine series of farm wagons made exactly to one-eighth scale from existing examples by Mr H.R. Waiting 1932–8, commissioned by Mr Wade. These show the two principal types, bow wagons from Wiltshire and box wagons from Warwickshire. These varied with the different loads that they had to carry and the land on which they worked.

Two models by Mr Waiting of the Magnet stage coach and of the Bath House Fly, a hand-drawn coach from Great Yarmouth.

Working model of a steam fire engine, c.1890.

A collection of children's prams, 1750–1900, some modelled on farm wagons, others on carriages of the period and one in the form of a hansom cab.

Wade's collection of 'bone-shaker' bicycles (1870–85) in Hundred Wheels

Hanging from the roof are:

A fifty-two-inch wheeled Ordinary or Penny Farthing bicycle of about 1890 with oil lamp fitted within the wheel.

Two wooden-wheeled Ordinaries.

A large model of a hundred-gun ship of about 1800.

A coach builder's model of an Indian state palanquin.

A collection of measuring wheels called waywisers or pedometers marked in rods, furlongs and miles. Eighteenth- and nineteenth-centuries.

Seventh Heaven

Seventh Heaven was perhaps Mr Wade's favourite part of his collection and contains many of the toys he had as a child before 1900. He wrote 'Seventh Heaven only to be attained in childhood before schools and schoolmasters have been able to destroy the greatest of treasures, imagination.'

CONTENTS

A small doll's house which belonged to Wade's mother.

Two wind toys, a soldier with two swords and a marine.

Seventh Heaven was one of Wade's favourite rooms. It contained many of his own childhood toys, a reminder of that idyllic time when the imagination is still free to roam unhindered

A model of a French three-masted lugger 'La Fantaisie' from Bordeaux.

A South African covered wagon.

A baby walker on castors.

A baby minder on a pole attached to the floor.

An early baby minder, used on board a ship to stop the child from falling over.

A mahogany and cane cradle, *c*.1800.

Several nineteenth-century embroidery samplers.

At the head of the Old Stairs, on the left, is:

Top Royal
This and the adjoining rooms are named after ships' masts, and represent their position in the house. They are devoted mostly to spinning, weaving and lace-making.

CONTENTS
A large collection of nineteenth-century coloured prints, cheaply produced for cottage decoration and often of religious or moral subjects.

A cobbler's bench and full set of tools used by Sam Thurlow of Yoxford, Suffolk, Mr Wade's home village.

Two glover's donkey clamps used to hold the glove when stitching.

Charcoal, Italian and goffering irons.

Lace-maker's lamps, lace bobbin winders, a collection of lace pillows, one on a stand, and an embroidery frame.

Top Royal and the adjoining rooms are named after ships' masts and also reflect their position in the house. Pictured here is the cobbler's bench used by Sam Thurlow of Yoxford, Wade's home village, and a collection of nineteenth-century prints

Treasure beyond measure,
Imaginative mind,
Magic key to open,
The Realm of anywhere

C.P.W.

Top Gallant

CONTENTS
Two warping mills, used to draw off the threads to the right length to set up the warp, or long threads of a piece of cloth, on a loom. One of these was used with the loom in the next room.

Two of the collection of mainly nineteenth-century spinning wheels (Top Gallant)

A collection of spinning wheels including examples of most of the varieties used in Europe, mainly nineteenth-century, also skein winders, bobbin frames and spinning chairs.

A turret clock by W. Jones of Abingdon, 1803. This type of clock, often used in churches, has no hands but strikes the hours. Mr Wade painted a scale on the wall to show the time by a pointer on the descending weight. The riddles about time are from the writings of Nicholas Breton, *c*.1600.

A collection of spring balances and steelyard weighing machines.

A white-faced tavern clock by King of Woodbridge, late eighteenth-century, without its case.

A horse measurer by W. Newton of Grantham.

A Black Forest clock, *c*.1820, with figures that strike the bells on the quarters.

A large hoist, similar to that at the head of the stairs, brought from the slaughter house in Broadway. It can lift 1 ton with a pull of 3cwt 37½lb.

Mizzen

CONTENTS
Many small tools associated with cloth making, including a large collection of fly and hand shuttles.

A great Welsh spinning wheel which is used without a flyer.

A hand loom from Sudbury, Suffolk, for weaving silk. It was in use up to 1922 when Mr Wade bought it. The material on the loom is not silk, but shows how it was set up.

Table with holes for pegs (bought as a music notation table for a blind person *c*.1840).

A box mangle or pressing machine, *c.*1850, from Chipping Campden. The box is filled with stones and the linen to be pressed is placed around the rollers, fitted with a reciprocating gear.

Ribbon and quill wheels for winding thread.

Several Black Forest clocks.

Over the door are portable medicine chests used by apothecaries, doctors and large households in the eighteenth century.

Old Stairs (Upper flight)
The staircase is of simple construction around a square well, probably built within the hall when it was subdivided *c.*1600.

CONTENTS
Over the stairwell is a wooden windlass from the Snowshill Arms.

On the upper window sill is a collection of rushlights and candle holders.

Two processional candle holders.

Two sets of Cromwellian armour, the one on the left has an original buff coat.

Two collections of beetles, butterflies and other insects arranged decoratively in frames.

A turret clock similar to the one in Top Gallant but *c.*1700.

Two machines for rolling lead window cames, early nineteenth-century.

Two hand-operated clockmaker's lathes.

A clockmaker's gear cutter, late eighteenth-century.

Ann's Room
This seems to be the upper part of the great hall of *c.*1500, the roof of which was retained when the floor and fireplace were inserted about one hundred years later.

The inscription over the door means you cannot conceal love or a cough. This refers to the secret marriage that occurred between Anthony Palmer and Ann Parsons, against the wishes of her guardian. Subsequently the court of the Star Chamber declared the marriage illegal.

Ann's Room, the upper part of the sixteenth-century great hall. The oak canopied bed dates from c.1700 and the limewood rocking chair from c.1800

CONTENTS
A collection of seventeenth- and eighteenth-century books, mainly religious and legal.

An oak canopied bed with rope mattress supports and holes for five corpse candles, *c.*1700.

Still-life with an earthenware jug and basket of apples, painting attributed to Jacques Linard (*c*.1600–45).

Interior with a woman, child and maidservant, painting by Richard van Bleeck (*c*.1670–*c*.1733)?

An oak rocking cradle, *c*.1700.

Two warming pans.

Two cottage wing-back rocking chairs, *c*.1800 (one in limewood).

A bracket clock with four figures that strike bells each quarter and a fifth that strikes the hour. This type of clock was cheaply made in the Black Forest in the eighteenth and nineteenth centuries and exported in large numbers for cottage use. They are known as 'Dutch Clocks'.

Behind the door is a large oak buffet, Welsh, *c*.1700.

Rangda masks from the Javanese theatre (Seraphim)

Far right:
An artist's lay figure sitting on a painted red chair (Seraphim)

An Italian carved chest dated 1698.

A Friesland bracket clock similar to the one in Zenith.

Two oak chests of drawers, one dated 1611, Spanish Vargueño (with fall front) and Papiliera travelling chests on top.

Seraphim
The panelling and box bed were put in by Mr Wade. The ceiling is similar to that in Ann's Room.

CONTENTS
Indo-Persian armour.

Two Spanish Papiliera cabinets standing on Jacobean chests of drawers.

A collection of Balinese and Javanese dancing masks.

A South German marquetry cabinet of architectural design, *c*.1560.

A collection of Indian and African musical instruments.

On the table are Indian ball censers, sea shells from the Indian Ocean and a collection of Persian lacquer.

Spanish Vargueño cabinet on a Pie de Puente (stand with legs).

Three Spanish carved plaster pictures of gateways at the Alhambra Palace, Granada.

Artist's lay figure.

Three Persian hanging lanterns of pierced brass.

A Dutch box bed in oak, dated 1680.

Music Room

The inscription over the door may be translated 'Man is carried to heaven on the wings of music'.

The instruments have been arranged approximately in the form of a small orchestra or band with the brass and percussion on the right, the woodwind in the centre and the strings on the left.

CONTENTS

A banjo, inlaid with Tunbridge ware, *c*.1870.

A keyed guitar and a lyreguitar, late eighteenth-century.

Three citterns or English guitars, *c*.1870. Four harplutes, *c*.1820.

Three hurdy-gurdies, one late eighteenth-century, two mid-nineteenth-century. A mandolin with mother-of-pearl inlay, late eighteenth-century.

A three-stringed double bass from Cheltenham Parish Church, late eighteenth-century.

Two eighteenth-century cellos.

Two bowed zithers to be played on a table, mid-nineteenth-century.

Two Irish harps, *c*.1820.

Flageolets, oboes, clarinets, flutes and a piccolo, *c*.1800–20.

Two walking stick flutes, *c*.1800.

Three bassoons, one with a copper horn, *c*.1800–20.

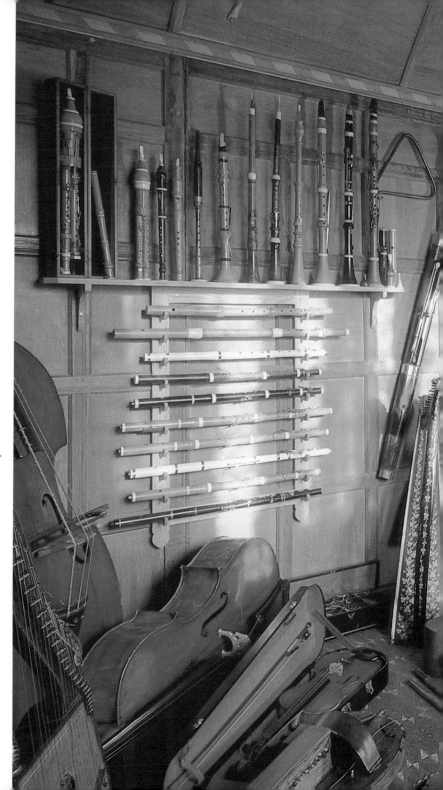

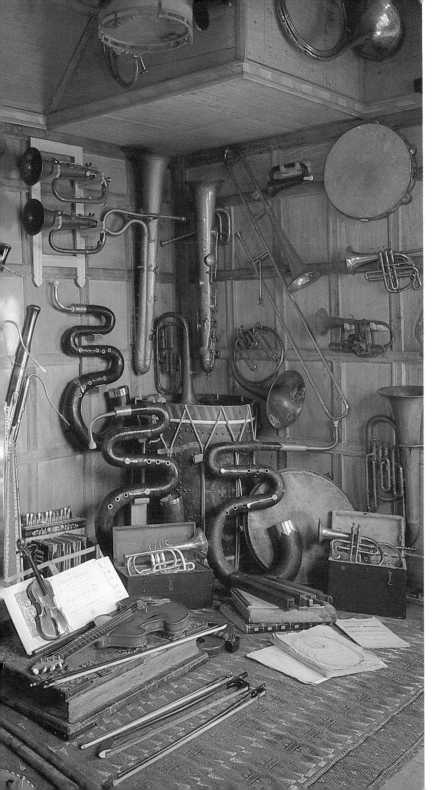

A bell from a buccin trombone, ending in a serpent's head, made in Belgium in the nineteenth century.

A French hunting horn and a coaching horn, nineteenth-century.

Two keyed bugles, *c.*1840.

Three serpents, late eighteenth-century to early nineteenth-century.

A bass ophicleide, *c.*1830.

Two cornopeans, one in a box, *c.*1850.

A silver-plated cornet in a box, *c.*1850.

An early trombone, late eighteenth-century.

A slide trumpet with silver mounts, *c.*1840.

Two tambourines, *c.*1795.

A triangle formerly used by the Snowshill Morris men.

Four pitch pipes for setting the note for a church choir, early nineteenth-century.

Several books of songs and music, early nineteenth-century.

A long drum and a kettle drum, late eighteenth-century.

The Music Room

Old Stairs (Lower flight)

CONTENTS
The lower flight contains:

A 'Parliament Clock' similar to that in Zenith.

A Flemish tapestry, seventeenth-century.

A set of leather fire buckets, some with the arms of Lord Henniker.

A fire insurance sign.

Salamander

The gallery is named after the lizard-like animal that is associated with fire. This contains a number of painted heraldic shields, including one painted on a large tortoise shell, also two Scottish basket-hilted sabres and a collection of footmen's staves and walking sticks.

Dragon

Dragon derives its name from the fire that Mr Wade often had burning in what was probably the great fireplace of the medieval hall, the upper part of the hall being Ann's Room. This room was for many years the kitchen of the house.

Around the upper parts of the walls are coats of arms of the owners or occupiers of the Manor from the Abbots of Winchcombe to recent times. These were made by Mr Wade and include the Royal arms over the fireplace.

Dragon, showing the great fireplace, coats of arms, suits of armour and long oak table of c.1650

38

CONTENTS

A three-quarter suit of German armour *c.*1600, the leg pieces added later.

A three-quarter suit of German armour with engraved breastplate of *c.*1540.

A collection of weapons. German two-handed swords, Portuguese swords, halberds and a fine German stag-hunting crossbow dated 1585.

Three-quarter suit of armour in Dragon, c.1600, to which the leg pieces were later added. Coats of arms hang on the upper walls

The window sill of Dragon, with a collection of keys, padlocks, brass cooking pots and a sugar cutter on a wooden stand

On the window sills are keys, padlocks, brass cooking pots and a sugar cutter on a wooden stand.

A portrait of Henry VIII, a contemporary copy of a Holbein.

An iron chest with complicated lock, German, seventeenth-century.

Glass demi-johns and a sack bottle from the West Indies standing on an eighteenth-century oak buffet.

A portrait of an unknown eighteenth-century Dutch girl.

A high-backed curved oak settle, *c.*1700.

Two German side-axes for shaping timber.

Over the fireplace are two English rapiers, *c.*1650.

Two weight-driven spit turners.

The great fireplace has a Sussex iron fireback with the arms of Henry VIII, two posset dogs, an iron chimney crane, two clockwork bottle jacks, two long faggot forks, a pair of bellows, a rotary bellows, a cage to hold claypipes to be burnt clean, a cage spit and, in front of it, a large copper dripping pan.

A long oak table, *c.*1650, and oak bench.

On the table are Italian marble and plaster fruit.

A large Spanish antiphonal, a hand-written church service book on vellum dated 1680, with musical notation and Latin text.

Nadir
This room is called Nadir from its position in the house, the opposite to Zenith. The inscription in gilt letters round the cornice is adapted from the writings of Nicholas Breton. ('A wise man is like a dial, that being set right by the sun keepeth his true course in his compass. He measureth time and tempereth nature, he employeth reason and commandeth sense and envieth none.') This and the wagon-vault ceiling were installed by Mr Wade.

CONTENTS
On the window sill is a Yomud tent bag, and a bronze figure of *A Mother and Children* by P. Dubois, late nineteenth-century.

A pair of Venetian lanterns, eighteenth-century, on either side of a German marquetry cabinet *c.* 1560.

A Spanish reliquary statue of St Teresa of Avila (1515–82), founder of the Order of Barefooted Carmelites, on a Spanish walnut cabinet on stand, *c.* 1700.

Next to the fireplace is an early eighteenth-century Italian cabinet in ebony with inlaid marble.

An Italian ebony and tortoiseshell cabinet *c.* 1700.

A French cross, fourteenth-century.

A square piano by Longman & Co., Cheapside, London, 1802 or soon after.

Passing through Dragon to:

Lobby
The original main door of the hall house of *c.*1500.

CONTENTS

A collection of truncheons including a Bow Street Runner's tipstaff. The crown unscrews to contain the warrant.

A collection of beadles', church wardens' and village guild staves including those of several local villages.

A set of wagon team bells fitted by Mr Wade as a door bell.

Visitors can now leave by the door, if open, or return to the front door and turn right to reach the Priest's House and the Garden.

Detail of Italian ebony and marble cabinet (Nadir)

The Priest's House

The cottage to the west of the Manor house was, as the name implies, a priest's lodgings in monastic times. It was later a brewhouse and had become a farm building by the time Charles Wade bought Snowshill. He converted the cottage for his own daily use, reserving the Manor house for his collections and entertaining. On the ground floor are his kitchen and living room. They are seen now as he left them in 1956 except for the installation of some electricity. There was a fire in the living-room grate winter and summer which always gave a bright and cheerful welcome. The hall porter's chair on the left was Mr Wade's favourite, where he would sit listening to *Much Binding in the Marsh* and *The Brains' Trust* on his battery-driven wireless. The cord hanging above the chair opposite leads through to his workshop where it operates

The expectant cat adds an extra air of domesticity to the kitchen

The living-room in the Priest's House

a pair of blacksmith's bellows, which are connected back to the fireplace to blow the fire.

The multitude of objects on the walls and ceiling are too numerous to list, but are mainly English domestic and farm tools including horse harness and an ox yoke. Over the fireplace is the original spit rack filled with Mr Wade's collection of roasting spits. There are also several weight-driven spit turners and an anti-poacher gun which is fired by a trip wire.

Upstairs is Mr Wade's bedroom, with a gallery along the west side that gives access to the windows. The balustrade was made out of a manger rail from an old stable in Framlingham, Suffolk. The large crucifix in the roof was made and painted by Mr Wade; in the corner is his cupboard bed.

The bathroom adjoins. Water was supplied by hydraulic ram from the stream in the valley and there was a boiler in the room below, which provided hot water and central heating.

In out-of-the-way corners, out-of-the-way people spring up. Open a certain green high gate, go down the garden path to a grey stone cot – the kettle is boiling on the hob, a wooden cat crouches by the hearth... the Master sits on a stool, whittling merry fairy folk. He carves them bold and paints them gay.

GRETCHEN GREEN, 1936

Wade's bedroom in the Priest's House. He made and painted the large crucifix on the far wall

YESU·FOR·YE·MODIR·SAKE·SAVE·AL·YE·SAULS·THAT·I·ME·GA

The Garden

Then did I see a pleasant paradise
Full of sweet flowers and dantiest delights

When Wade arrived at Snowshill the garden
was far from a pleasant paradise: 'Nettles
covered the slope from the very walls of the
house right down to the Kitchen Garden,
strewn with old iron, broken crocks and
debris. The only wall was that to the
orchard on the south, which follows the fall
of the ground. Springs had formed a
treacherous swampy morass in what is now
the lower garden.' But Wade immediately
saw the possibilities, and asked his former
colleague at Parker & Unwin, M.H. Baillie
Scott, to help him design a new garden.
Wade was clear about the principles he
should follow:

'First the house required a secure base to
stand upon, to lose the feeling it gave of
being about to slide into the depths of the
valley below, so terraced levels and retaining
walls were necessary.

'A garden is an extension of the house, a
series of outdoor rooms. The word garden
means a garth, an enclosed space. So the
design was planned as a series of separate
courts, sunny ones contrasting with shady
ones and different courts for varying moods.

'The plan of the garden is much more
important than the flowers in it. Walls, steps
and alley ways give a permanent
setting, so that it is pleasant and orderly in
both summer and winter.

'Mystery is most valuable in design; never
show all there is at once. Plan for enticing
vistas with a hint of something beyond.

A path through one of
Wade's colourful herbaceous
borders, with the dovecote
beyond

Have broad effects of light and shade.
Unbroken stretches of grass are a great
asset, do not cut them up with flower beds
as is so often seen. The contrast of the deep
and sombre tone of the yew with the vivid
green of the lawn, changing in the evening,
to lights of gleaming gold between the
creeping shades.

'Indeed a delightful garden can be made
in which flowers play a very small part,
using effects of light and shade, vistas, steps
to changing levels, terraces, walls, fountains,
running water, a statue in the right place,
the gleam of heraldry or a domed garden
temple.'

All these features can be found at
Snowshill, bar the garden temple, and,
although Wade may have been more
interested in garden design than in

The teak statue of
St George, mounted on the
wall of Wade's cottage

Pink and yellow roses climb
one of the walls of the
Snowshill garden

Bacchus fountain in the Armillary Court

individual flowers, there is much for the plantsman to enjoy. The garden is also the first in the National Trust to be run entirely organically.

The short stretch between the road and the front gates is planted with yews, laurels and snowberries. Across an open expanse of lawn is the house itself, against which are trained *Ceanothus x delileanus* 'Gloire de Versailles' and *Clematis montana alba*. In summer tubs of seasonal bedding plants sit on the flagged terrace to the west of the house. Adjoining the west terrace is Wade's vine-covered cottage, on which is mounted a painted statue of St George carved in teak in 1922 after a fifteenth-century French original. This once rang the bell, connected to a clock, in the room beyond. The bell-cote and much else in the garden is painted in Wade's preferred shade of turquoise blue.

From the west terrace steps lined with columnar yews lead down into the Armillary Court, which has a gilded sun dial on a stone column at its centre.

On the level below is the Well Court, which again takes its name from the central feature, an ancient Venetian well-head. Cream waterlilies flourish in the small pond and the raised bed that runs along one side of the court is crowded with varieties that would have been familiar to medieval plantsmen. Wade converted the former cow-byre on the north side of the court into a garden house with a summer bedroom on the upper floor, and created a little shrine to the Virgin Mary in a gable on the roof. The building, which is smothered in vines, contains a Flemish chariot dated 1839; two manual fire pumps of around 1850 by Merryweather; and a Double Gloucester

cheese press. On the west side of the court is the dovecote, which is thought to be late medieval. It may originally have had four gables or a simple pyramidal roof, but the gables have apparently been rebuilt. There are nest boxes for 380 birds in the thickness of the walls which are now home to white pigeons. In a recess in a nearby wall is a zodiac clock or *nychthemeron*, picked out in Wade blue and gold.

The lower garden house contains some of the models from Wade's imaginary Cornish fishing village of 'Wolf's Cove', which once stood around the large pool, but which have now been moved under cover to save them from further deterioration. John Betjeman was so impressed with Wade's creation that in 1932 he devoted an article in the *Architectural Review* (complete with photographs and plan) to an elaborately mock serious description of the village. Betjeman's evocation of a vanished merry England where the motor car, and even the railway, were kept at a safe distance, must have struck a powerful chord with Charles Wade. Only in the last paragraph does Betjeman emerge from his reverie to admit that he is describing simply a half-inch scale model.

The Well Court